The Child Golfer - A Parent's Guide

The Child Golfer - A Parent's Guide

By
Terry L. Glatt

With Foreword by
Mrs. Julius Boros

TechLeader Publishing

International Standard Book Number: 978-0615892610

Photography by Marlene Glatt

childgolfer.com

To my son, Dylan ... for the gift you are. DLD, always!

And to my wife, Marlene, Mommy Caddy ... thank you.

Contents

Foreword

I've been surrounded by golf my whole life. My late husband Julius Boros is one of the top 50 PGA Tour players of all time, including two wins at the U.S. Open and a PGA Championship. I watched my children grow from child golfers to touring pros, including my son Guy who also won on the PGA Tour. My dad was a golf pro. Now I watch my grandchildren developing from child golfers into junior golfers. Oh, and I play too!

As a daughter, wife, mother, grandmother, and golfer myself, I can tell you this book is a much needed guide for parents. The information and experiences you'll find in The Child Golfer are really not available anywhere else. Though there are many sources of information about golf instruction for children and buying equipment for children, this is the first time I've seen a book written to help golf parents with what they have to know and do.

The parent of a young eight year old golfer for example must wear many hats. They need to learn the rules and how the game is played in order to not only teach their child, but to keep them on pace during a tournament. The parents must help the child find the distance and club to play, as well as teaching persistence and sportsmanship.

Teaching correct habits is very important for new golfing parents. The wrong grip and swing can become bad habits. The parents of a child golfer should try to find a PGA teaching professional for lessons, or even a children's group lesson or clinic. The fundamentals are key, but there is much more to helping your child golfer.

In addition to the rules and fundamentals, parents have to keep their child golfer confident, keep them having fun, keep them swinging within their range, and finding their natural setup and rhythm.

The Child Golfer – A Parent's Guide is especially helpful for parents of golfers starting under 10 years old. Believe me, it gets hard to tell an eleven year old what to do … they need to be on their own. The Child Golfer will help parents know when to and when not to. I remember my son as a junior golfer used to play in a Pee Wee Tour in Orlando. My husband and I would watch some parents basically do everything for their child, even lining them up for a putt. That is very wrong for a developed junior golfer, say older than eleven, but, for a five year old, that is what a parent may have to help with. Some young golfers start at two years old with plastic clubs and that's not too young to build in good habits, like the grip and attitude.

I have known Terry for years. Our child golfers have had the opportunity to play together in a number of the children's golf tournaments in South Florida. Terry is certainly an experienced Daddy Caddy and well known in the area. His son has grown steadily in competitive golf and plays quite well. Terry is absolutely qualified to help parents with what can be a challenging thing to do.

When Terry first told me about his book I immediately got it. I have seen many parents struggle with their new role of caddying and coaching their child golfer. The Child Golfer teaches parents how to get their child started in golf, how to get them into tournaments, and how to caddy for them. Tasks like planning the day, keeping score, keeping pace, managing the rules, handling the weather, and being a golf parent can all be quite challenging, especially for parents who don't have a golf background.

The golf is really only part of it. Being a parent adds a dimension to caddying that all parent coaches can relate to … it's often hard to coach your own child. The one on one nature of golf, their age, can intensify this.

Terry has written a simple to read, well organized book that will leave new Daddy Caddies, Mommy Caddies, Uncle Caddies, and Pop-Pop Caddies comfortable with how to help their child golfer. Without a good source of instruction for parents, many will not be comfortable enabling and supporting their child in the game, and for this reason may choose not to. I hope The Child Golfer – A Parent's Guide will help grow this wonderful sport of golf by making it easier for more parents to get their children started, armed with good information. Enjoy the book, enjoy your child golfer, and as Julius would always say, remember … "It is a game!"

Armen Boros

Introduction – Start Here

So you're thinking about golf for your child. Let me offer a resounding, "go for it!" Whether it's your own interest, or your child's interest in golf, you should definitely take the next step. Hopefully you bought this book to help you down the road to giving a wonderful gift to your child, and to yourself. At the time of publishing this book, my child golfer is ten years old. He started playing when he was three years old. The meaningful memories and lessons golf has given our family through our son's play have been amazing. It's a great sport, with great people, the great outdoors, great challenges, and fantastic experiences and lessons for a lifetime. It's just great!

According to a recent statistic, there are over twenty-six million golfers in America, six million of which are below the age of eighteen. There are many good reasons why golf is such a popular sport, perhaps the most important is that it can be enjoyed until a ripe old age ... and at a very young age. What's interesting is that many fantastic golfers, including my son, won't even know what it's like to learn to play golf. Many learned to play before the age when their recollection starts, which is said to be around six years old. By the time my son was six, he was already shooting in the low forties for nine holes! The truth is many golfers will be playing even after their recollection fades.

Another wonderful thing about golf is that it is enjoyed by males and females alike. There are nearly six million female golfers in America. What is so special about all of this is that we have given our son the gift of possibly enjoying great time together with his wife in their old age, perhaps playing golf with each other into their sunset. Who knows? For all the reasons you can find between three and one-hundred and three, go for it.

My son also loves football. He loves to follow the NFL players and teams and games and stats. He loves to play football as well. We encourage him, and I encourage you (as will college coaches) to keep room for other loves and interests for sure, especially academics. One observation I pointed out to our son is, "What do professional athletes in other sports want to be good at during their spare time and after their career? Golf!" Many professional athletes wish they could play as well as our child golfer.

We had to learn a lot. We did not come from a country club background. I play golf, but with an average handicap of about twenty-three, so this will not be another golf instruction book. You should seek a PGA Professional Instructor for that. We watched many parents struggle with getting into golf, just because they did not have the background either, but wanted it for their child. The need for a parents' instruction manual became apparent to me after we were experienced and saw the deer-in-the-headlights look on many new parents who came to golf tournaments for the first time. Other parents often express interest for their child and a fascination for our accomplishments in supporting our son's golf. Most don't know how to get started, where to play, how to find instructions, what happens at a tournament, how to keep score, or even how to rent a golf cart!

This book is intended to be an instruction manual for the parents of a child golfer, and we mean a child younger than ten, even as young as three years old. I hope this book helps you bring golf into your child's life, and your life too. Please take the next step and let The Child Golfer, a Parent's Guide help you along the way. Good golfing! Enjoy and cherish every moment with your child golfer.

Chapter One – The Gift

Football, baseball, soccer, dance, volleyball, basketball, even gymnastics, these are all what we might call "Osmosis Sports". American children will absorb these activities just by being a child in America. Certainly, to excel in any of them will take focus, training, and practice, but, children will more than likely have a chance to learn and play them just in the course of being a child.

On the other hand, golf is a sport you have to learn on purpose. For the children who have the good fortune to grow up in a country club, golf may be an Osmosis Sport. However a majority of children will have to be exposed to golf intentionally. The sport is wonderful for the child and the whole family. With a long tradition of persistence, integrity, sportsmanship, focus, and life lessons like no other, so much so that, in my opinion, golf should be a college requirement!

The other sports have an advantage of practice by osmosis. Recess, the playground, after school, summer play … all will be filled with chances for children to play and hone their skills, many times right outside your door. Golf needs special effort, equipment, time, and lessons. The special effort and time is yours too, not just your child's. Good golf requires instruction, it's not easy. I once had a professional caddy tell me, "golf is hard, and we're not supposed to be good at it." As a recreational golfer I can tell you, he is right. Therefore, practice time, course time, and instruction are all very important. If you don't live on a golf course, you cannot get away with throwing a ball out the door and say, "see you at dinner." With a three to ten year old golfer, they'll need your commitment too. From observation, the parent's commitment to golf is more like tennis than football.

In addition to the time and effort, there will be costs. Clubs, balls, lessons, greens fees, entry fees, shoes, clothes, and travel are all things to keep in mind as you consider your child golfer's present and future. These costs don't have to be high. Some parents will spend more than others. Keep in mind it's really hard to wear out a golf club at this age, so pre-owned is definitely a good option. The good news is, while there is a minimum spending commitment of some sort, spending more doesn't necessarily yield better results.

Golf is a gift, and, at the risk of sounding cliché, it's a gift that keeps on giving … possibly for life. In the spirit of a gift being something you can't or wouldn't give to yourself, golf is a gift from you to your child. More than the time and money, the game gives the opportunity to learn so many values. These values are difficult to put in order of importance.

One such value is dedication. All sports require dedication, so I don't intend to demean those. However, to be good at hitting that little ball straight, far, and as few times as possible, the child golfer must be dedicated to practice. Raw talent will help no doubt, and may get the child golfer ten or fifteen good shots, but most assuredly not forty-five, forty, or thirty-five as would be hoped for in a junior round of nine holes.

Golf teaches a lot of focus; not just on the shot, but on the mental part of the sport, the rules, the etiquette, the day, the course, the hole. It all comes down to the shot, but for the beginning golf family, the rest of the list all requires focus from the start.

What part will the sport play in your life? Do you know the rules to be sure your child golfer learns and plays by them? During play, do you follow the etiquette that 'is' golf? Have you prepared for the day; registered on time, rested, a practice round, good nutrition, travel? Do you have what you need for the round; equipment, drinks, snacks, rain gear? How will you play this hole; lay-up, go for it, left, right, chip, putt? It all sets up the shot, every shot. Which club, the setup, the grip, the swing, ball contact, the finish? The focus required is quite amazing and the child golfer's ability to step up to the ball, clear their head, and demonstrate that focus so many times is really quite amazing; in most cases, better than the parents by far.

Golf is a game of rules, and decisions on those rules. The United States Golf Association (USGA) is the main governing body for the rules of golf in America. Every year they publish the extensive set of rules, and decisions, that affect play. One of the most important gifts of golf is teaching your child to play by the rules. Golf is not golf without its rules. Believe me that there will be a lesson or two in there for you as well!

Resilience is another of golf's gifts. In a junior round, there will be thirty-five (hopefully), forty, to fifty or (hopefully not) more opportunities for frustration and disappointment. A bad shot, a bad hole, a bad round … they will all happen. I once read that the young Tiger Woods' best trait was his ability to leave a bad shot behind. Any golfer will tell you that, aside from the basic skill set, the ability to quickly put a bad shot or hole behind you is the number one most important trait of a good player. Teaching your child to have this resilience is a fantastic gift. Keep in mind that part of this gift is bouncing back from a good shot! Yes, sometimes, taking a good shot with you to the next can be detrimental. That same pro caddy once told me, "be sure never to focus too much on the lows, or the highs, and there will be plenty of both in the game. To be a good golfer, you need to plot a steady course over the long haul."

Courtesy; you've heard it I'm sure, "golf is the gentlemen's game." It's true. Like the rules, golf is not golf without the courtesy. One of the most profound moments as a young golfer's parent was when I realized that, unlike most sports available to my son (e.g. football), he was learning, not to compete <u>with</u> his friends against others, but compete <u>against</u> his friends. We found that with the other competitive sports, being on a team and competing with your friends against others was the underlying theme (albeit a good one). In golf, we saw our son compete <u>against</u> his friends, one on one, yet, congratulate a good shot during play, console a bad shot, and immediately leave the game behind when it was over. This gift is the ability to separate, yet combine, high-level competition and friendship. The fact that the child golfer learns this at such a young age is fantastic. You'll look at your son or daughter and realize that is a gift few of their peers will have at their young age. Some of the best photos from tournaments are of the seven year old threesome walking ahead side by side down the fairway, smiling and chatting, while in the heat of a tournament.

Mark Twain's famous assessment of golf as "a good walk spoiled" well is just not true. Junior golf gives your child, and you, the opportunity to take some of the best walks of her life. Whether it is a local tournament or a US Kids Golf Championship, the courses are always a great place to be. Getting your child out for the walk, teaching them to respect the course by fixing divots and ball marks, picking up a piece of trash, seeing the birds and other wild life, are yet more of golf's great gifts to your child. Frankly, more often I would thank him for giving these gifts to me. These are moments to be savored and will be a wonderful part of your child's memory.

Let me share one of those moments please. I don't remember the final score, or which tour it was, or even who our playing partners were. What I do remember is my nine year old son pulled his tee shot left and the ball landed under some trees near lots of roots and leaves. Of course I was caddying. When we arrived at the ball for his second shot, we saw it would be a very tough one. The ball had a playable lie, but was near roots, which could be dangerous, and under the canopy; you don't want to bang a root as a shock injury could result. He said, "Dad, I want to play it." With the right focus, it would be a safe stroke. There is always the option for a golfer to "take an unplayable" as per rule 28, at the cost of a one-stroke penalty. The shot was about one-hundred yards and had to flight up over roots, stay down under tree branches, and clear water for about eighty yards to the green. I still tear up with pride as I remember the confidence, focus, poise, know-how, and determination that little guy showed. After two or three practices with his seven iron, he put the ball back in his stance, leaned left, looked once, kept his head down and pitched that ball through the bull's eye and onto the green. The result was incredible by any standard. However, I unwrapped that gift before the ball even left his club. The result was just the ribbon. I'll never forget my son at that moment.

The list of golf's gifts would not be complete without including the people. In our experience, junior golf includes a full variety of children from all backgrounds. There is a pleasantly surprising lesson in diversity in junior golf. One thing for sure, the values the game teaches bring out the best in each and every one of the children who play. We've made some good friends from all walks of life thanks to golf. It's likely our son will have some of those friends for a long, long time.

Junior golf from age three to twelve is really focused on learning the values, the skills, the rules of play, and building the basis for more "hard core" competition with the potential for college play and maybe more. During these years, you don't, you can't, know where it will go. Perhaps college play, maybe just play with dad or mom on the weekends? However, no matter what the future holds, to watch the child golfer receive all of the game's gifts at such a young age is literally breathtaking at times. This experience is the game's gift to you.

Chapter Two – Getting Started

This is Mr. Wood. Here is his friend, Mr. Iron, and here is their friend, Mr. Putter. Make a bun with your hands, and put the hot dog in the bun to help Mr. Wood put the ball in the hole. At age three, this was our son's introduction to golf. We had the good fortune of having an after school program that had golf as a choice. The first step is to find a program that provides a fun introduction to the basics. No matter at what age your child's introduction occurs, make sure it's fun. The fun will give her interest its best chance at surfacing. From that after school program, we realized our son had an interest in golf. It was certainly too early to assess any real talent, but he certainly had an interest. It is worth noting that, at age three, the golf clubs are plastic. Yep, that little plastic set you see in the toy store is where it all begins for the very young child golfer. Remember to keep in mind it's all about fun. Let them choose their club (it really makes no difference), focus on the shot, take turns, knuckle bumping or high fives, and introducing little competitions.

The next step is their first set of clubs to hit a real ball. We bought ours after that semester's enrichment program was over. The set we bought may have cost thirty dollars at Toys 'r Us. This set was the right size, as no "real" junior golf set was small enough. These clubs had steel shafts and metal heads. There was a wood, an iron, and a putter that came in a little blue bag. Our son was just shy of four years old. Please keep in mind that a four year old with a steel shafted golf club in her hand can be dangerous! Be sure to supervise the activity very closely, especially if there are other children involved. We have friends who put their four and five year old boys in a weekend golf program. By accident, the older boy took a back swing with the younger boy behind him and struck the four year old in the face. He required stitches in his lip and will be scarred both physically and mentally. Watch young children with clubs very carefully and be sure the program coaches are well organized.

Depending on your budget, you may decide to find a golf pro who teaches children, or at least an age-appropriate golf program for children at school or at a golf course. If you're inclined as I was, the good news is basic swing and putting instruction is not hard to learn. The even-better news is, for this age of four years old, you don't have to be good at golf yourself. You can learn the basics enough to help your child get improving results. The key is still … keep it fun.

As an introduction, keep in mind there are four main parts to a golf swing: the setup, the back swing, the through swing, and the finish. These four parts can be taught to a young child golfer. For the setup: have her straddle the ball, club behind it, and count to three before the back swing. For the back swing and through swing: after counting to three in the setup, have them say "peanut" in the back swing and "butter" in the through swing, or "Coca" "Cola", or anything they have fun saying that has a tempo. For the finish: our son "won" a trophy during his golf after school enrichment class at two and a half. He was very proud. We always told him, and still do … "finish like your trophy." Visuals are better than words at this age and they can see the trophy and imitate it.

I found that four was too young to "officially" get out on a course, greens fees were not justified, keeping any pace of play would be impossible, and it was just plain too much for him at this point. So, we used to walk on to the practice facility at our local municipal course. This approach is very cost effective, in our case free. It was also very convenient in that we could do it almost anytime we wanted. We started with putting. Ten minutes tops, unless he wanted more. I'd challenge him from close, attainable distances, usually less than six feet. The swing thoughts I learned and taught him were, keep your eye on the ball until it is gone, and swing back and forth smoothly. I want to make a note here that, at that early age, his interest and some talent were apparent. What was also apparent then and remained a challenge for us was getting him to slow down. He was so eager to hit the ball and get it into the hole, he would rush his set up; more on that later.

As his putting improved and he started consistently two-putting from outside six feet, we moved off the green with the iron. Keep in mind we are still using the "toy" steel set. Here the challenge was to make par: a chip on and a two put. First we started just off the fringe, then increased the chipping distance as he improved.

It wasn't long until my son asked, "What about Mr. Wood?" At that point, I took him to the practice tee with a small bucket and introduced him to driving. The swing thoughts are the same … swing smoothly and keep looking at the ball until it is gone (head down). All the while, I was reading and learning about a good golf swing. A side benefit was that I improved my game a bit. An added component to the driver swing for him was to brush the grass going back. I would show him a sweep back from the ball along the grass, then, swing smoothly and keep your head down. Again, as with putting and chipping, never more than ten maybe twenty minutes, unless he asked to stay. I was always aware of attention span and keeping it fresh, short, and sweet.

The finish may be the most important part of a good golf swing. Without a good upright balanced finish in mind from the start, it's very difficult to have a good swing. Our friend, another daddy caddy would remind his golfer, "dirty toe," so he'd remember his finish. By the way, you'll hear the term swing thought a lot in golf. These thoughts are the little reminders in each part of the swing. Go to a trophy store and buy a small inexpensive golf trophy and give this prize to your child golfer early. The trophy will help to explain a good finish without words, time and again! "Finish like your trophy." This trick worked very well.

Speaking of prizes, please let me share another tool I employed along the way, and still do. We established "par prizes" for our son. A par prize is a small prize for making par. At this stage, we defined par as a three strokes, a chip onto the green and two putts. What quickly became apparent for us was that this was also a wonderful tool to teach earning and saving. We allowed him to accumulate prizes and two small prizes equaled a medium prize and three small prizes equaled a large prize. My wife and I discussed par prizes and together we decided we like the idea for us. We felt that even for pros, prizes are a part of the sport. We established the value of a small prize at five dollars or less. This amount of five dollars for a small prize was okay with us and our budget, but truthfully to a four year old, is somewhat arbitrary. If you choose to employ par prizes, certainly choose a value, or even non-monetary prizes, that work and feel right for you. Children that young have no concept of dollar value, it's the prize itself that motivates them.

Now, I said five-dollar par prizes worked within our budget, but, very quickly, that train left the station and was chugging really fast down the track! He was walking away with two and three prizes each session. So, with due explanation and request for his understanding that, "I have to buy dinner too," we had to change par to two strokes, a chip close and one putt. Well, I have to tell you, he was making pars again in no time. We created a monster; and we were happy about it. He was getting good at golf very quickly and wanted to play a lot. He was also very proud when we made our trips to the store for prizes, and, if he had none "stored up", he was eager to play to earn some. Par prizes stayed with him for a long time, albeit with some adjustments as he improved.

One day we were at the chipping green and, lo and behold, he aced one … yep, a hole in one. An ace was bound to happen, but boy, when it did, he looked at me as if he did something wrong. He just didn't know what to do! I nearly cried. This was another gift from him to me that I will cherish forever; that look on his face was priceless. That was the moment I decided he was ready for the course. Oh, and I bonused him an extra prize for the ace.

Chapter Three – His First Round of Golf

One of the greatest days of my life ... walking into the golf pro shop with my four year old son, golf clubs on the cart, paid the greens fees, ready for our first round of golf together. It was a tough course, the Doral Blue Monster. My son shot a seventy three and beat me by one stroke. "He is going to be the next Tiger Woods for sure!" ... ok, so, a dad can dream can't he? Neither of us were anywhere near Doral, nor the seventies. Actually, I took him to Palm Aire Country Club, a public executive course near our home. Their Sabals executive course was a par twenty-nine nine-hole course with par threes around one-hundred yards or less from the forward tees.

I made up pars for him. He was driving about sixty to eighty yards. So the rule was set so that if he needed two shots to be on, the hole was a par four, three shots on, a par five. For example, a ninety-five yard par three would take him two shots on and two putts to "par" for a prize. Couldn't say from that round if he was actually going to be the next Tiger Woods, but boy did we have fun. He earned three or four prizes that round. The boy was playing golf, and frankly he was pretty good (I thought!). I later learned in Tiger's book, that his dad set pars for him as well. I was proud to learn that Mr. Woods and I came up with the same scenario to encourage success in our boys' golf play.

The par four, hole number four, on the Sabals course was three hundred and sixty five yards. When we arrived at the forward tees, he looked at me with intimidation and said, "Dad, it's so far." I decided, instead of skipping the hole, we would set his par at eleven. Yes a par eleven! My thoughts came from some reading I had done, in golf, you never quit. I did not want to have the hole beat him. Well he shot a birdie ten that first time and earned a prize for better than par. Since then by the way, it has always been our favorite hole. He has since birdied it for real with a three.

We played Sabals almost every weekend for a few years. That hole four became my gauge to measure how he was progressing. Once he was able to reach the hole in three for a shot at "real" par, I knew it was time for the next step. The next step was to seek a pro. We needed a pro for two reasons, first, to be sure dad was building him the right swing, and second, to learn from someone what to do and where to go next. The pro we found was Steve Conte at Conte's Golf Academy at Palm Aire. Mr. Conte is married to Michele Conte who toured on the LPGA, and both were teaching. The better news is, they have a son my son's age, so they had a first-hand perspective on the mind of a six year old golfer.

Chapter Four – Accept What You Don't Know and Get a Pro

Working with a golf pro was the right move at this point. You'll want to consider it too. The good news is that I had "done good." Mr. Conte complimented us on a good swing. Dylan had the basics, but, certainly would benefit from some tweaking in his swing. As proud as I was, I was also humble enough to know what I don't know. Steve taught the basics, well, like a pro. GASP; grip, aim, stance, posture, were the first set of fundamentals. I remember watching my boy's swing and thinking, "you know, he looks like a little pro." His swing had all the trimmings of a pro's swing. That straight left arm, head down, a "dirty toe" balanced trophy finish, were all there in his swing.

There are many references to golf as a game of inches, and they are all true. Building the basics with the help of a pro will go a long way. There are lots and lots of teaching golf pros out there and hopefully you can find one that fits your budget and goals. A putt missed by an inch equates back to a fraction of an inch error in the golf set up or swing. A fairway missed by a few yards translates back to a similar fraction of an inch in the setup or swing. A good golf swing is kind of like electronics, you can't just guess, you have to study it on some level to get it right. I am not a golf pro, so this won't be a golf lesson book. However, I am a golf student, and I will try to share what I've learned in hopes to help you find your understanding enough to help your child be a better golfer.

The good news is, the golf swing is a lot easier to understand than to do. So you should be able to listen and learn from a pro enough to observe your child's set up and swing and remind them of the pro's teachings to keep them on track. Don't be afraid to ask the pro to help you at least understand the things she is trying to accomplish with your child so you can reinforce them during practice.

We had a boy on our tours that was a great young golfer. His dad was an athlete through college and also coached baseball. When his son decided to pursue golf as a priority, I never heard him mention a golf pro, though I believe he visited one a couple of times. His son definitely had natural talent, and together they were both good students of the swing, and it worked for them. The natural talent didn't hurt. With a small investment in lessons with a teaching pro, you can get some direction on various parts of the set up and swing you need, then carry it forward to your own work with your child golfer. However, I truly suggest regular "observations" and recommendations by a pro as they see things we can't. Bad set up and swing behavior creeps in very quickly and turns into habits that are hard to reverse. Stay on top of it as much as you can.

More and more pros and courses are recognizing the growth in child golf and offer child golf instruction and programs. To find a teaching pro, call the courses nearby and ask to speak with the pro shop. Another place to look is www.PGA.com and click on their Find Instruction link or Junior Golf link. You may want to ask the tournament directors and other players who they would recommend. It's a special pro that can teach child golf versus adult students.

Chapter Five – Tournament Golf

Tournament golf is available for children as young as four years old, usually in a six and under flight. US Kids Golf[1] is one example organization with junior tournaments in many parts of the country for children from four to fourteen. Tournament golf is a great choice at this point. One of the nice things about tournaments is that it offers something for all personalities. Some children are very competitive and confident; some are shy and less competitive. Watching the different personalities is quite a treat for the parents. If approached from the right perspective, tournament golf can feed the competitor as well as build confidence and teach persistence. Most experienced folks we spoke with all said competition is low on the list of reasons to enter tournament golf at this age.

The top reasons we found to enjoy tournament golf are: 1. learning how the game is played, 2. learning the rules, 3. learning persistence, 4. learning sportsmanship, 5. learning etiquette, 6. having fun. All of these experiences are valuable regardless of results. We found, like with other sports at this age, the parents are much more concerned about results. For the child golfer, it's the journey, not the destination. In fact

---

[1] www.uskidsgolf.com

this is true for most amateur golfers. Another benefit of tournament play is that, well, they are playing. Otherwise it's up to you to independently make the time and get to them to the course. The more they play, the better they get. Tournaments are a great reason to get out and play. I look forward to walking as my son's caddy in every tournament I can.

We met some really nice people at tournaments. Most folks involved in golf tournaments at any age are a pleasure to know, and there is a variety. Meeting new friends for you and your child is a nice benefit of this wonderful sport.

A tournament is an organized event where golfers are organized into groups, or flights. Flights are usually by age, for example Under 6, 7-8, 9-10, 11-12, etc. However, as in the Junior Golf Association of Broward County[2], in some competitions the children are grouped by performance. A tour is a series of tournaments by the same organization, many times at different golf courses. A tour is usually capped by a championship tournament which may or may not span more than one round (day). For example, there may be a two-day championship with nine holes per day.

In a performance-based tour, the golfers all start in the same flight and the lowest scoring players are advanced to the next

---

[2] JGA.org, in South Florida

flight. For example, your golfer may start in the F flight. If she places in the top two or three (depending on tour rules), along with getting her trophy, she advances to the next flight, E. If she finishes the season in E, she will start in E the next season. In this fashion, golfers of like skill compete against each other. Our golfer played against other golfers who were fourteen because he was as good a golfer as they were as they started playing much later than he did.

In age-based tours, children compete against others of the same age, usually also for trophies. In these tours, golfers of the same age play against each other regardless of skill level. US Kids Golf for example, holds "Local Tours" in many parts of the country. These are age-based tournaments. Here in South Florida there are two or three tours in the summer and one or two at other times throughout the year. We have the US Kids West Palm Summer Tour, the Miami Fall Tour, etc. Our US Kids Golf tour director provides "never give up" medals for the children outside of the top five. Fifth and fourth place get a different colored medal, and the top three on the leader board win trophies. They do a really nice job running tournaments for the children.

The leader board is the listing of players in order of low score, i.e. the leader with the lowest score is listed first and the rest of the players listed down in order. As each pairing in each flight finishes, the scorers fill in the scores on the leader board. Once the flight has completed, trophies are awarded. In most junior tournaments, a first place tie is decided by a play off. A play off is where the tied players go back to the course and repeat holes until there is a winner. Ties for second place and higher are usually settled by comparing the score cards of the tied players in a score card playoff, in most cases starting with the last hole and going backwards hole by hole. If the tour has a points system, ties for second place and higher will usually share the points together, but the tie breaker determines who gets which trophy. However, the winner of a first place play off, gets all the first place points as well as the trophy. For example, in a second place tie, where the points for second and third are 20 and 10 respectively, they both get 15 points, though the winner of the score card playoff takes home the second place trophy. A tie for second, as example, will show as T2 in the results on the leader board. If there is a points system for example, the points will be tallied throughout the tour and sometimes a tour cup is given for the player with the most accumulated points; this is sometimes called player of the year. Some tours will have top three or even top five players of the year awards.

The tours use a web site for providing tournament information, dates, registration, tee times and results. Once you find a tour for your child, you'll need to sign up ahead of time as a user, and as a player, to be able to register for tournaments. A sign-up fee is typical in addition to a fee for each tournament. After you sign up as a member of the tour and register and pay for a tournament, you wait for an email or web site posting of acceptance, your tee time, and pairing. The tee times are usually posted two days to a week prior to the tournament. Beware that registration for a tournament will often close as early as a week prior to the event. You won't be able to register after that. Some tours allow late registration for an extra late fee.

Your pairing tells you the other players who will tee off with your golfer at your assigned tee time. The tours are usually run by a local pro who is the tour director. The tour director will assign pairings of two, three, or four players depending on the roster for the flight. You'll never see a pairing more than four. Keep in mind that tournaments are guided by rules that are usually posted on the tour's web site. The rules are sometimes called local rules, so as not to be confused with the USGA Rules of Golf. Be sure to familiarize yourself with the tour rules. In some cases, the player must pass a rules test or attend a rules session, in order to be able to sign up for the tour.

Most tournaments are stroke play tournaments where the player's strokes are added up for a score (more on scoring later). A variation of tournament stroke play is match play. Match play is where a player competes in a match up with another player and the score is a comparative score, not an absolute stroke count. If a player holes out in fewer strokes than their competitor, she wins the hole. So even if it takes one player ten strokes and the other eleven, the player with ten strokes wins that hole. There is no score kept other than an accounting of how many holes each player wins. As example here, if a player wins five holes in a nine-hole tournament, they are said to have won 5 and 4. Since there are only four holes remaining their competitor could not possibly win, even if they won all four. More on match play scores later in the scoring chapter.

Sometimes, to reduce the time a tournament occupies a course, there will be a shotgun start. This start is where pairings are sent out, to start one pairing at every hole, at the same time, instead of everyone starting on hole number one in sequence. If your starting tee is number four, your golfer will tee off at hole four finish on hole three, so the whole field rotates around the course at the same time, and finishes about the same time.

Another tournament variation is the scramble or best ball. This format is usually reserved for team play in charity tournaments and fund raisers, however, best ball is also good for beginning players. In the best ball scramble, each player in the team tees off, then the best shot is selected by the team and each player plays from there. This process continues until the hole is completed and the score is kept for each team. Best ball format is also good for young players to build social skills and team work. The reason a scramble is good for beginners is that it filters out bad shots and usually everyone gets to play from a decent shot. Often there are rules applied where the team must play at least one drive from each player, or other similar requirements.

Junior golf is on the rise in many parts of the country. I've observed an increase in the number of participants at events over the years. The increase in popularity means that more and more pros and courses are offering junior events and lessons.

You'll likely find an event near you by calling some of your local golf courses. An easier way to find child golf events may be simply using Google to search for "junior golf tournament <city>" where city is your town or a city near you. In place of tournament you can also try tour and association. Check to see if they have flights suitable for your golfer.

US Kids Golf is a large organization that sells junior golf equipment and apparel and also offers a huge network of junior golf tournaments. They have local tours with a series of tournaments, regional tournaments, national championships, and international events too. Their tournaments website is www.USKidsGolf.com. We have played in over a one hundred US Kids Golf Tournaments and our local tour director runs a very nice tour. Below are a few other links that can help you find a tournament. Clicking around some of these will lead you to other tour sites too. Just be sure to look for the events that have a flight for your child's age, or performance level.

Other sources of tournament info are AGJA Tournaments Reference at http://www.ajga.org, Junior Golf Scoreboard at juniorgolfscoreboard.com, and The First Tee at thefirsttee.org.

The PGA Junior League at pgajrleaguegolf.com is a match play format league for junior golf formed by the PGA, much like little league baseball. There may be teams in your area.

Another good way to find golf activities for your child golfer is to ask other parents at events you attend. Be sure to ask the children who play well as they are likely playing at a good number of events.

For the child golfer, tournaments are a great way to learn the game, build confidence, and make new friends. Let's take a look at tournaments in more detail.

Chapter Six – Her First Tournament

How exciting! You're all signed up for your golfer's first tournament. Let's take a look at what the day might look like. Plan to be at the golf course the day of a tournament at least an hour prior to your tee time. The competitor will need to sign in at a table somewhere upon arrival. After you're signed in, go through a warm up. Some children's tournaments include range balls in the registration fee, others charge for a bucket of balls; usually it's just few dollars. We'll talk about warm up and what will work for your golfer, but, arrival one hour early should allow for a thirty minute warm up after ten minutes for signing in. Then ten minutes for a bathroom stop if needed. Get to your starting tee ten minutes before your tee time. Being on time in this fashion is a critical habit to form from the very beginning. Keep in mind that penalties may be assessed to your player if he is late to the starting tee.

Don't forget the number one purpose for golf at this age is fun! The parents have a much easier time forgetting this than their kids. The time before the tournament can be a great social opportunity for the young players. Try to keep this in mind and find your own mix of warm up focus and fun. We found that heading out to the practice tee first to hit no more than two or three balls per club type, for example, 9 iron, 7 iron, 3 hybrid, 3 wood, and driver, could take roughly fifteen minutes. After about eight minutes of chipping green warm up with a wedge, it's off to the putting green. The practice green is where they will usually putt together and even have little contests among themselves. Each family will have different motivations; some are more serious than others. Find your own objectives for the sport, but keep in mind the value of this social interaction and play time on the practice green. This time has value as it allows the player to relax and ease into the competition. I would be remiss not to mention, the joy of watching my young golfer on the practice green "with the boys". Those memories are a new gift each and every time.

Sign in with the starting official at the first tee. She will introduce you to your playing partners and hand out score cards. Each player must have unique markings on their ball. Usually a Sharpie® or other marker is used to make an easily identifiable mark on the ball such as the player's initials. The players will identify their ball to their pairing to ensure there can be no confusion during play. Keep in mind that relying just on the ball brand and number is not acceptable, as according to USGA rules, a player must be able to identify the ball as specifically hers.

At the younger ages, for example seven years old and younger, there may be one score card for the whole pairing, with a parent volunteering to keep score for the players. Otherwise, each player gets a card and then they swap score cards so that each player's score is recorded by a playing partner. At ages eight and nine, most often, a parent-caddy will mark the score card on the player's behalf. Starting at ten years of age, some tours will require the player to mark the score themselves. Some may not even allow caddies.

Most tours allow spectators and have specific rules about them. Cart use, behavior, attire, and contact with players are usually very specifically defined in the tour rules. Spectator carts are invariable restricted to the cart path only. To rent a cart, go into the pro shop, pay a rental fee, and get a slip. Then take that slip out to a cart attendant and he will give you a cart to use. I've never seen a course allow more than one person per seat, which in most golf carts would be two people per cart. Some courses have a loose policy regarding children and we often see mom with two siblings in a cart, but pay close attention to the rules, as your golfer may be penalized for rules violations by their spectators. Also pay attention to the tournament rules regarding the players riding. Sometimes riding between holes is allowed for the young ones, but most often they must walk.

Before we go into what happens during a tournament, let's take a look at keeping score.

Chapter Seven – Keeping Score

Many times, parents arrive at a tournament and they are handed a score card with no idea how to use the card, let alone keep score in golf. I've heard moms in this position actually express fear. They find themselves in a position to do something they have no idea how to do. Unfortunately, scoring can be a source of conflict between parents at this age, as you will find parents who are very serious about the score. Let's be clear, scoring in golf is very specific and a very important part of the game. Being serious about score is a good thing, especially for teaching your child golfer the game. However, be serious about your golfer's score, but don't be too serious about others' scores. The more you know the rules and how to score, the more comfortable you'll be in situations on the course. More importantly, the more you know the more you can help your golfer learn to play her game.

Let's go over how to score. There are a lot of rules in golf, so how to score is a very large topic. I'll break scoring down as simply as possible. You will have a nice introduction on how to score here so that at a minimum, you won't have to experience that fear of the unknown during your first tournaments as caddy.

First, any attempt to advance the ball to the hole by hitting it with a club is called a <u>stroke</u>. Basically, a golf score is comprised of adding up all the strokes it took the player to <u>hole out</u>, i.e. stroke the ball into the cup on the green according to the rules of play. Every attempt to advance the ball, whether or not the ball is actually struck as intended, is to be counted as a stroke. For example, a swing and a miss that was intended to advance the ball is counted as one stroke. However, accidentally tapping the ball off the tee while setting up is not a stroke, as the player was not attempting to advance the ball and the ball was not yet in play.

The tee, or <u>tee box</u>, is the where the first stroke of each hole occurs. Every stroke from the tee to the cup is added up and recorded as the score for that hole. On the score card, there is a box numbered for each hole. The score for a given hole is written in the box for that hole number. At the end of the round, the hole scores are added together as the total score for the round. Just to be clear, the lower the score the better, the goal is to hit the ball into the cup with as few strokes as possible.

You will also see the yardage and par number for each hole on the score card. The yardage indicated on the score card is from the middle tee position to the middle of the green. The tee and cup positions are varied from day to day to even out course wear and tear and vary the nature or "play" of each hole a bit. Distance and measuring will be discussed later.

The <u>par</u> number is the number of strokes considered standard for the hole. The standard for any hole assumes two putts. Therefore, if you subtract two from the par number, you will know how many strokes it takes to be on the green <u>in regulation</u>.   Pars are universally three, four, or five, and of course the par rating is dependent upon the length of the hole. Often you will hear, "on in two with a two putt." Thinking of the score this way may help as an easy way to keep score for the hole. You count how many strokes to get onto the green, and then how many putts to sink the ball into the cup, then add them together for the hole's score.

At the end of the round the hole scores are all added together to find the total score for the round. Usually the scorer and player are responsible for the accuracy of the hole scores and the total score is added up by the scoring official at the scoring table. Teach your child golfer how to keep score early. Later they will need to pay attention to their score and their playing partners' scores too.

Often a golf score is described relative to par. Adding up the individual par numbers for every hole gives you the par for that course. Many times par for a course is thirty-six for nine holes, and seventy-two for eighteen holes. Some courses are par seventy or seventy-one. Stating a score relative to par would be how many total strokes different from par the score is. So a score of seventy on a par seventy-two course would be stated as "two under" or -2. In a multi-day tournament, scores are added together for all the days. So for a three day tournament on a par 72 course, if you shoot a seventy each day your tournament score would be a 210. Par for the tournament would be three times 72 or 216. So this score would be six under par for the tournament, or -6.

If a rule is broken during play, often the rule calls for a penalty. For example, if the flag stick is touched by a putted ball, there is a two-stroke penalty. So, if the ball goes in the hole on the fifth stroke, and touches the pin, the scorer should put a seven in the box on the score card for that hole, thereby adding two strokes to the hole's score for the penalty. As a side note, always remove the pin from the hole when putting on the green!

Another note on the score card ... do not put any markings on the face of the card. Only hole scores and signatures are allowed on the face of official score cards. If you plan to use hash galaxy marks or any other markings, use the back of the card or another piece of paper. The player can be penalized or disqualified if the card is inappropriately marked up.

Match play scoring is different than stroke play. In match play, the player who holes out with fewest strokes wins the hole. It doesn't really matter how many strokes, as long as it was fewer than their opponent, they won the hole. By way of example, if player A wins the first hole his score is 1-up. If the players tie for the rest of the holes, player A wins the match 1-up and player B loses the match 1-down. Tying a hole is called <u>halving</u> the hole. Another example: if after five holes, player A won three holes and player B won two holes, player A is again 1-up since she won three holes and player B won two. In this example, if player A wins hole 6, she will then be 2-up since she won four and B won two.

Note that you can get to a point in the round where there are not enough holes left for a losing player to come back and tie the round, even if they won all the remaining holes. As example, if player A wins all five of the first holes, she will be 5-up going into hole six. However, even if player B won holes 6 through 9, that's only four wins and they would finish with player A 1-up. In this case, the match is declared won by player A with a score of "5 and 4"; that's 5-up and only 4 left to play, no chance for B. Yet another example, if player A is 3-up after hole even, she will be declared the winner with a score of "3 and 2"; 3-up with only 2 holes left.

In match play, if the players are tied by either halving every hole or both winning the same number of holes, they are said to be <u>even</u>. Another term you'll hear in match play is <u>dormie</u>. If player A is up by the same number as holes left to play, the match is said to have gone dormie. Dormie means player A has assured herself at least half a point in a match tournament as they will be even at the end if player B wins all three remaining holes. In this example, if the tournament is a one-round tournament, then dormie really has no meaning as the players will likely play off until there is a winner. Dormie does have meaning in multi-round match play like the Presidents Cup, Ryder Cup, and Solheim Cup, where points are added up to win; a half point will count. As an example if player B is 4-up after five holes ("4 and 4") in a nine hole tournament, he is said to have taken the match dormie, since the worst that can happen for him is to finish even, or all square, if player A wins the remaining four holes.

Though handicapping is not used in competitive golf, it may be useful for you to have a cursory understanding about handicapping in amateur golf. A golfer's handicap index is an indicator of how they typically score. So a handicap of 20 loosely indicates the player averages about 20 strokes over par for an eighteen-hole round. I say loosely because the handicap is not that simple, it is calculated using a formula that considers the difficulty of courses played.

The purpose of a handicap is to allow players of different skill levels to have a meaningful competition. Otherwise a golfer with handicap of eight will likely always beat a golfer with a handicap of twenty. The handicap levels the playing field. A player's handicap index is used to calculate the course handicap for any give course. At each course there will be a conversion table or program that will calculate a course handicap for the tees to be played and the player's handicap index. For example, if the course handicap is 16, the player will get to take a stroke off their score for the sixteen most difficult holes on the course. The <u>handicap line</u> on the score card has numbers 1 through 18 where 1 indicates the most difficult hole; note that any hole may be the most difficult, so if hole six is the most difficult hole, then its handicap number will be 1. The handicapped score is also known as the <u>net score</u>. So, a six on a handicapped hole is counted as a net five. Essentially, if the player's <u>gross score</u> is 96, their net score would be 80. One last note on handicap; if your course handicap is 20 for example, you get to take two strokes off your score for the two most difficult holes and one stroke for the other holes.

Now that you understand how to score, let's get into a tournament.

Chapter Eight – Tournament Play

You learned above that a parent usually keeps score in tournaments for young juniors. The person keeping score is called a <u>marker</u>. In some junior tours, a parent volunteer is asked to be the marker for each pairing. The marker walks along with the pairing and marks the score for all the players. We need to teach the junior golfer that ultimate responsibility for a player's score lies with the player, even at this young age. Your child golfer will sign for her score at the end of the tournament. You will delight in your child golfer's ability to know what their score is during play. If you are a marker, you should confirm the hole scores with each player after each and every hole.

In most tours, instead of a single marker per pairing, each player is given an individual score card. The players are then asked to swap cards to keep another player's score. In this case, the card will have a row for the players score and a row for the marker's score. Sometimes the player's row is labeled "self" and the marker's row is labeled "partner". This labeling can be confusing, but remember self refers to the player whose score card it is, the marker is partner.

Golfers at this age will likely be allowed, and often required to have a caddy, usually a parent. If you are the caddy then you will likely be the marker for the other player and your child as well. The official side of the card should not have any marks on it other than the hole scores for the player and the marker, and perhaps the marker's name. As a tip, you may consider using the back side of the card to use tally marks for tracking strokes as each hole progresses. At the completion of every hole, confirm the score with each player and mark the score on the official side. A good idea is to confirm the scores with the other caddies too, hole by hole. Waiting until the end of the round to confirm scores may be asking for trouble. Get your player in the habit of confirming the scores right after each hole as they are walking to the next tee box. You will also want to review the scores at the end of the round too. Be sure you hand the score card to you golfer with the correct scores for them to review with the official at the scoring table. The markers (officially the junior golfer, not you) will review the score you kept with the player in front of the official. The marker and the player both sign the score card and turn it in. Each player will sign twice, once as a marker (on another player's card) and once as a player (on their own card).

We learned an important lesson at the scoring table after playing the Junior Honda Classic. I verbally read through Dylan's scores hole by hole with the marker and agreed on each hole and the total of 47. Assuming all was good, after getting his card from the marker, Dylan signed his card and

Chapter Eight – Tournament Play   53

turned it in. The leader board showed a 48 for Dylan. When I asked to review the score card, the marker had written a six on hole nine (resulting in 48), yet he knew and agreed it was a five during our verbal review. Somehow the marker made an error after verbally going through the scores with me and handing the card to Dylan.

Even though we all told the official the correct score for hole nine was five, and even though the marker agreed it was his error, the official would not correct it. Once the card is signed and submitted, it is official and cannot be changed to the benefit of the player. The lesson is: always check the scores on your official score card before signing the card. Though it was disappointing to have the wrong score posted, this was an unforgettable lesson for both of us to learn at this time.

You should familiarize yourself with the rules of golf. Knowing when to add a penalty stroke is very important. Each player should be taught responsibility for their own penalties. The grownups must teach the young golfers to follow the rules and score accordingly. Two scores can only be comparable if they are both scored the same way in accordance with the rules.

Depending on the how the tour directors, parents, and children you play with approach it, tournament scoring may be stressful; it shouldn't be. At the heart of golf is honor and integrity. The best approach to scoring is when each player applies the rules

The Child Golfer – A Parent's Guide

of golf to their own play. As your child grows through experiences in junior golf tournaments, you will both experience different temperaments in your playing partners. The best experiences will be had when the players and caddies focus on their own score and application of the rules to their own play.

Though college golf let alone professional golf may be a long way away, you rarely see a player at those levels focus on another player. Golfers at those levels have grown in the game by learning to be focused on their own play ... not another's play or score. The best approach to teach your child golfer is to learn the rules and be diligent in applying them to their own play, proactively. You'll appreciate how wonderful competitive golf is with players who know the rules and focus on their own play. Keep this in mind when you run across the parent, and it will most likely be the parent, not the child, who focuses on your golfer's play. Make your priority the example you set for your young athlete and keep the fun high on the priority list, not the outcome.

Pace of play is important and tracked during tournaments. Usually the standard is fifteen minutes per hole for junior tournaments. A pairing should finish nine holes in two hours and fifteen minutes or less. Pairings may be penalized if their pace of play is too slow. Sometimes a question of how to apply the rules for proper scoring can slow the pace of play. For example a lost ball, or a hazard, can slow the pace of play.

Don't hesitate to call an official over if there is ever a question of how to apply the rules, whether raised by your golfer or a partner. The officials are trained to make a call quickly and effectively. If there is not an official within reach, there are two rules that can help you score accurately while keeping your pace of play: Rule 27-2 Provisional Ball, and Rule 3-3 Second Ball. Both of these rules will allow you to play another ball and to determine which ball will "count". Learn these two rules and apply them carefully. The player must declare the intent to use these rules and be sure to resolve them prior to signing the score card. Keep in mind the USGA normally allows five minutes to search for a lost ball, and everyone can help.

Here are some pace of play habits to learn and teach your child golfer:

• No more than 40 seconds to complete a golf shot, from the time they arrive at the ball to the time they are in their swing finish. This same 40 Seconds includes all the Daddy Caddy help with alignment and setup too! This is especially important on the green.

• No more than 3 practice swings.

• Find the distance and select the club early while her partner is taking his shot so when he is finished, she is ready to take her shot.

• Evaluate the putt early as soon as they are on the green.

• One he addresses the ball on the green, putt within 8 seconds. This habit is probably better for his putting too.

- Walk directly from the green to the next tee. Enjoy the social opportunity for the players, but keep them tracking to the next tee on pace.
- Put your golf bag at the "exit" of the green. Don't leave it back at your chip shot. This will avoid having to walk back all the way to get the bag when finished the hole; simply walk off the green and on to the next tee.
- Learn how to use Rules 3-3 and 27-2 to play a second ball or provisional ball to keep up pace of play.
- Leave the green right away and check scores etc. on the way to the next tee. Don't hold a meeting on the green after a hole!

In our experience the two worst culprits for introducing undue delay are lost balls/hazards and putting. The putting green may be the worst.

You child golfer must learn how to determine distance on the course, even if you have a distance measuring device like those described in the Equipment chapter. Every course will have distance markers on every hole. In most cases there will be red, white, blue, and gold stakes or markers of some sort. Red is one-hundred yards from the center of the green. White is one-hundred and fifty yards, blue is two-hundred yards, and gold is two-hundred and fifty yards. Sometimes the cart paths have markers on them and often sprinkler heads are marked with distance as well. Sometimes there will be mid markers too, for example a red and white marker is one-hundred and twenty-five yards.

An important note here about the rules and scoring from a Daddy Caddy's perspective … try hard not to get caught up in the rules, or the score for that matter. In other words, don't take it all too seriously. Some people have a hard time with this; I admit I did at first until I learned. Do not make the rules or the score the focus of the game. The rules are there to be sure scores all have the same meaning. Remember to keep the focus on the fun and the play. Lead by example. The outcome of any given tournament at this age really doesn't matter. The effort is what matters. Teaching the child golfer to focus on their own play according to the rules will set them up for a long and happy golfing career, with good friends. There are few prouder moments than when your eight year old calls a penalty on himself! You will gush with pride and admiration of the integrity and honor demonstrated by that little person.

Weather can turn an already challenging round of golf into a really tough situation without the right knowledge and approach. The first time my son played in the Publix-Doral Classic in Miami we endured torrential down pours and wind for every hole through eight. Everything was soaked. We lost two umbrellas to wind damage. Did I mention we were soaked? We may as well have jumped into a pool with the golf bag and I assure you we wouldn't have been much wetter. This tournament was our first big one. Leaving the call regarding play to the officials, we wanted to teach our young athlete to hang tough. I was not sure that was the best decision at the time, but it is what everyone else was doing.

There were moments when we all were questioning what was happening and why we were putting our children through that. I have since thought hard about this and being a parent is first. We'd all like to think everyone involved in the tournament is responsible and will always make the right call. It's a bit tough to say, and a bit antiestablishment, but keep in mind tournaments at this age really don't mean much beyond the experience, learning, and fun. Make whatever call you are comfortable with as a parent and for the well-being of your child. You are supposed to listen to the officials and that's what you want to teach, but at the end of the day, follow your heart. If we had decided to leave the course without official decision, our golfer would have taken and WD, or withdrawal.

As we were walking to the ball after our tee shots on hole nine, the lightning horn sounded. The lightning horn will sound if there is lightning within striking distance, said to be about fourteen miles or closer. Golf will not usually halt unless there is lightning, rain and wind alone won't do it. The rule is, if the horn sounds, the players should mark their ball, leave the ball and their pull cart, take their clubs and find shelter. Spectators with carts are encouraged to provide rides to the players to take them to safety quickly. Courses usually have shelters out on the course. Go to one of the shelters if the club house is not near. Players are required to stop play if the horn sounds, or risk disqualification.

In this particular tournament, the director decided play could not resume. They cancelled the day's play. That was hard. We endured nearly nine holes of weather, only to finally have the horn sound and all that grueling play cancelled. We wondered why they didn't do so earlier. However, our child golfer learned from a very valuable experience. This became a lesson that many young golfers won't have when they start to compete. The experience contributes to the seasoning of a seasoned golfer. As a side note, he played quite well. The rain and wind forced him to really focus on the ball and his shot.

While we were there, our child golfer learned what to do when the horn sounds, how to play in bad weather gear, to follow the rules and the officials, how to deal with disappointment during a tournament, and how to manage a wet and windy course. We wouldn't have chosen that experience on purpose, but it taught us a lot.

After that Publix-Doral rain out, we had others. We learned that a round can be halted for rain even if there is no lightning. The greens are the gauge. If the greens flood to the point where you can't putt, you don't have to putt. You should get an official to say so though, but it's likely they'll sound the horn to stop play. There are two relevant rules here: casual water (USGA 25-1) and lift clean and place, which is a local rule declared by the tournament director. Casual Water allows for relief through the green if a ball or stance is affected by standing water. Lift clean and place allows a player to mark her ball, lift it, clean it, and place it back down. Sometimes the local rule allows for placing the ball a within a club length, sometimes within a score card. Be sure to confirm with an official whether lift clean and place is in play.

Chances are your young golfer will get to experience playing in the rain. Weather is part of the game. Approach your tournament with the right gear, the right knowledge, and the right attitude, and enjoy the golf, even if it's rainy golf!

Some terms you'll hear frequently during a tournament are through the green, out of bounds, lost ball, hazard, play it as it lies, honors, furthest from the hole, play a provisional, and ready golf. In no particular order, here's a bit on what they mean.

Through the green means the whole course, except the tee and the green of the hole being played and hazards. Some rules may be applied this way. For example, a director may allow lift, clean, and place through the green. That means the player would be allowed to lift, clean, and place through the hole, since you are always allowed to do so on the green.

Golf courses have out of bounds areas usually marked with white stakes and/or lines. If you hit a ball out of bounds, you need to play it over from the original spot. Some junior tournaments play out of bounds like a hazard to keep pace of play moving, so double check the tournament rules. Any time you can't find your ball, even if you think you see it but don't know for sure, there is a penalty and you have to play it as a lost ball. Our son actually hit a ball into a palm tree and we could see it but could not identify it by his marking. He had to play it as a lost ball. Hazards are the exception, if you can say with certainty that a ball went into the water, you may play it like a hazard. Sand bunkers are called hazards too. Bunkers are pretty obvious but look for red stakes and lines to mark other hazards.

Play it as it lies means just that, where ever and however it lies, that's how you play it. This is the norm for golf play. Rule 28 allows for playing an unplayable ball, but with a penalty. Furthest from the hole decides who plays first, through the hole. On the tee box, the player with the lowest score on the previous hole has honors and tees off first. If two players have the same lowest score, the one who had honors most recently keeps honors. Sometimes in junior tournaments the director will call for ready golf. This type of play is where honors and furthest from the hole are abandoned and the players play as they are ready, usually with a nod from the others in their pairing.

Play a provisional means to play a second ball according to rule 27-2. This rule is important to know to keep up pace of play if you believe a ball has been lost out of bounds. Rule 3-3 allows for a <u>second ball</u> to be played if there is doubt about how to proceed and an official is not nearby. These rules are confused by child golfers frequently since they are similar.

Tournament play for children is a lot of fun when approached from the right perspective. You will find a broad range of skills in the tournaments. As example, ten year old boys nine-hole scores in South Florida can range from even par 36 up to the sixties. There could be players who have played a hundred tournaments and others who are participating for the first time. The diversity is great and the children all usually have fun. The ones who don't have fun are the ones who take it too seriously.

I think it's important to close this chapter on tournament play with some insight on getting the best out of your young golfer. After your commitment to act as a parent first and keep fun and effort as the priorities, you'll still want them to achieve. Keep in mind tournament time is not the best time for teaching or learning. Instructions have a really good chance of being interpreted as criticism.

If you observe your golfer as a parent during a number of tournaments, you'll start to see what makes them tick. Try to leave instructions and lessons for practice time and focus on encouragement and always finding something good about every shot, or at least every hole. Focus on their effort, not the outcome. As they get older and better, cut them loose a bit.

Let your golfer determine their own distance and club, don't help so much with alignment. Leave them alone on the green. Sooner than later they have to play on their own. Work towards that goal during tournaments to give them their best chances later in middle school and high school.

Chapter Nine – Golf Attire

Unlike the Osmosis Sports, golfers don't usually wear a uniform. However, proper dress is expected at all golf courses so there is a uniform of sorts. Golfers are expected to wear a collared shirt, usually a golf shirt, tucked in, with a belt. Some high neck sports shirts are ok. Hats should be worn with the bill forward. Shorts are allowed. Jeans material is not acceptable. Females generally can leave their top un-tucked and are not expected to wear a collar. Golf attire is a great opportunity to let your child golfer express some style and have some fun. Take a look at John Daly and Ricky Fowler to see what I mean. Keep in mind that for both sweat and rain, dry-fit clothing is the best choice, i.e. not cotton. All the above holds true for caddies, and generally spectators as well. It can be a challenge at times to find child-sized golf clothes. US Kids Golf offers a line and you can check with your local golf superstore. The popularity of golf amongst children has not fallen on deaf ears in the sports apparel industry and choices are out there and increasing. You may want to consider tennis clothing as a source as well as there seems to be a good amount there in sizes that can work well for golf.

Golf shoes are important, though some children play in sneakers. If your budget allows, get a proper pair of golf shoes for your child golfer. Golf shoes offer anchoring stability for a better swing and moisture protection which are both important to good golf. Generally you can find junior golf shoes for much less than adult shoes. They are on sale a lot too.

Don't forget a hat. Protection from the sun is critical and a hat is an important step. If your child sweats, then a hat with an absorbent band will come in handy. Don't underestimate the value of a hat in your golfer's excitement to play the game. Hats are big in junior golf. I also recommend sunglasses. A lot of pros don't wear sunglasses, and in fact you'll see many who wear them backwards in order to satisfy a sponsor. However, three or five hours in the sun definitely calls for eye protection. Be a parent first, get a good pair of sunglasses that have good lenses and offer proper UV protection so the optics don't affect the child's perception and their eyes are protected.

Chapter Ten – A Primer on Golf Clubs

I have met many parents, my wife included, who see golf in their child's life, yet don't know anything about golf. Golf is an attractive activity for many reasons, even to those unfamiliar. For those of you who don't know an 8 iron from a clothes iron, here is a basic primer on golf clubs. Starting from the bottom up with respect to distance in general, the clubs order like this:

- Putter
- Lob wedge
- Sand wedge
- Gap wedge
- Pitching iron
- 9 iron
- 8 iron
- 7 iron
- 6 iron
- 5 iron or 5 hybrid
- 4 iron or 4 hybrid
- 3 iron or 3 hybrid
- 7 wood
- 5 wood
- 3 wood
- Driver

Note that the USGA rules only allow fourteen clubs in the bag of a tournament player. They can be fourteen putters if you want, but fourteen is the limit. Some players mix the various clubs, some may have a 5 iron but a 3 hybrid, some many will not use a 7 wood, and some may not have hybrids at all.

The Putter is the club that is used on the putting green. Most people are familiar with a putter at least from miniature golf. The irons, lob through 3 iron, are used off the green. Usually the lob is for just around the green and the 3 iron is for the longest distance. There are shots where a little chip onto the green with a 3 iron is a good call. Keep in mind what I am saying here is in general and each club can be used in a variety of shots. Hybrids are a mix between woods and irons, but usually thought of and used more like an iron. Hybrids are great clubs, and many pros are carrying them in their bags. You child golfer should swing hybrids instead of longer irons like a 3 iron. The hybrids are known to be much easier to hit than the low numbered irons. My son's best club is a 6 hybrid with thirty-one degrees of loft, which is close to a 7 iron's loft. We call this club "the money club" since he usually has good results with it.

When thinking about irons, picture the ball flight, and think high and short through low and long, from the lob wedge through the 3 iron respectively. The lob is intended to pitch up high, and land soft with little roll, but not go far; for example for close shots around the green. The 3 iron will go far and relatively low for the distance, in shots from the fairway out for example 180 yards from the green.

To help you remember think low and long for low number irons. So a 6 iron is longer than a 9 iron since 6 is lower than 9; the lower the number the longer the shot. Woods, which are usually metal these days, are the longest clubs in general. Just like with the irons, the lower the number the, longer the shot. A 7 wood is not as long as a 3 wood since three is a lower number.

Every club has <u>loft</u>. Loft is the angle of the club face. If you look at a 9 iron for example, you can see the face has a lot of loft, the 3 iron in contrast has a steeper face. The higher numbers are said to have a higher loft, the ball pitches up in the air more. So high number, high loft, low number, low loft/long shot.

The "1" wood is the <u>driver</u>. No one calls it the 1 wood though. There used to be a 1 iron, but it was a very hard club to hit. You'd be hard pressed to find anyone still carrying one. The driver is generally only used on the tee with a tee and is the longest of all clubs. A <u>tee</u> is the little pin used to set the ball up off the ground for the driver. This is only allowed in the tee box at the start of each hole. In general, for players up to seven years old or so, a putter, a sand wedge, a 7 iron, a 3 wood (fairway wood) or 3 hybrid, and a driver will get them started nicely.

Chapter Eleven – Choosing Clubs and Equipment

The good news is junior golf equipment is quite affordable compared to adult golf equipment. There are a number of brands out there that offer junior golf clubs, balls, gloves, and shoes. TaylorMade®, Nike®, Callaway®, US Kids Golf®, and others offer clubs that are designed specifically for juniors. I am not an equipment expert, but I can tell you what we experienced. I hope to offer some insights from a practical perspective. The theory on golf clubs is hard to nail down. Finding one right answer is even harder to do, and no one would commit to the direction we should take. Everything we could read was sales oriented as there were not any junior equipment testing-based reviews that we could find.

The classic story is about the youngster that starts with their dad's clubs cut down. One common theme we heard is that this isn't the best route. There is a characteristic of a golf club called swing weight. Don't confuse the swing weight of a club with its overall weight. Different combinations of shaft length, shaft weight, and head weight result in different "feels" when swinging the club. Picture the same club head on a six inch long shaft and a six foot long shaft. The two will clearly feel different while swinging. If one or two of the parameters is changed, the swing weight will change. Cutting the shaft changes its length and weight so the swing weight of the club will change. Also, shortening the shaft changes its stiffness. You might picture this easily if you again think about a two shafts of the same type where one is really long and one is really short. The short shaft would feel stiff and the long one would feel more "whippy". Cutting a shaft down will make it act stiffer which in turn will prevent the little snap ("release") at the ball that is need for distance. Without this release, the theory is, your child golfer may tend to <u>block</u> the ball to the right (for a right-handed player) since the head won't always release properly, thereby keeping the face of the club to the right a bit. Junior shafts typically have more flex to accommodate their shorter length.

In the beginning we found the clubs didn't make much difference. Getting to good contact with the ball was the priority, of course while laying the foundation for a good swing. We started at three years old with a toy set of steel shafted clubs. Within a few months we bought an orange set from US Kids Golf.

The problem we faced as our son progressed was finding the swing weight, overall weight, and stiffness values that were "right" for our child golfer. Of all the clubs and observations we made, four things stick out. The first is that we found some junior clubs to be too whippy, the shaft was not stiff enough. Our junior was always athletic and was able to swing the club pretty fast for his size. We could see the club flexing and he had trouble keeping his shots straight. The second observation that stands out from our experience is club length. Some junior clubs were too short. A short club caused our junior to stand too close to the ball which caused his swing to be too upright, again preventing consistently straight shots. The third observation is the overall weight of the club. The child golfer has to swing the club perhaps 40 or more times in a round. The weight of the club can make a difference here, you don't want them fatiguing. Also, we found some clubs were too light and prevented a smooth tempo because he could swing the club faster, "less smoothly".

Perhaps the most important fourth observation we made about club selection which had the biggest impact on our golfer's performance was excitement. The clubs that had the most impact on our player's game were the ones that made him excited to play. He played more, he practiced more, and his enjoyment and fun increase with his performance.

US Kids Golf has done a great job as the leader in junior golf. They have really integrated play with equipment and teaching in their approach for juniors. The US Kids equipment system is smart, as it offers a growth path from the youngest players to teens who are ready for adult clubs. Their system is color-coded for different height/length clubs. As your child golfer grows, they grow up through the system. US Kids also offers an advanced series which is geared for players with faster swing speeds.

We had the occasion to play with Jack Nicklaus' grandson in some tournaments around South Florida, and Mr. Nicklaus caddied for his grandson on a few of those. After one tournament in West Palm Beach, Mr. Nicklaus gave some pointers to one of the players and we listened intently. The biggest thing we heard is that your arms should hang naturally and comfortably during the setup. We took this away from that experience and apply it to both the golf swing and the clubs. So, if you're looking for maybe two thoughts to keep with you regarding clubs: 1. buy clubs for your child golfer that fit him most naturally, and 2. buy clubs that excite her, so she will be excited to play and practice.

Keep in mind that golf clubs take a long time to wear out. Pre-owned or used junior clubs are definitely worth considering. I can tell you first hand that we passed along some fine sets of junior clubs as our golfer progressed to new clubs. Sources like eBay® and craigslist®, as well as word of mouth, may yield some fine clubs for your junior golfer at a huge savings. Don't hesitate to explore these sources as you may end up with much better clubs than a new-club budget would allow.

A little bit about golf balls may be useful. The theory that may be the most interesting is about the <u>compression</u> of the ball and the ball <u>cover</u>. The compression of the ball indicates how easily the ball will deform when struck by a club head. The faster the club head is moving, the more any ball with deform, or compress; somewhere between a rock and a sponge. Since the club-head speed of a junior player will be slow relative to the industry, a low compression ball is, in theory, the best bet as it will have more spring off the club face for better distance compared to a harder ball. The cover of a ball generally determines durability and spin (or "feel"). The more expensive balls usually have a urethane cover. The rest usually have a Surlyn cover or some similar plastic (polymer). The urethane cover is less durable but provides more feel around the green. The others are more durable and have less spin, or less feel. Urethane covered balls are more expensive, so keep this in mind as well.

For a child golfer, a low compression Surlyn covered ball may be, in theory, the best choice. However, aside from the theory, you may again want to choose what excites them to play and practice. The difference the theory makes at this age can easily be trumped by the excitement your player has when playing a particular ball. Don't underestimate the value of the emotional part of this game. Playing the same ball his dad or her favorite pro plays will likely go much further toward improving their game at this age.

Get your child golfer used to playing with a glove; left hand for right-handed players and vice versa. They will play with a glove later and it makes little sense putting it off until then, unless a glove is an absolute deal breaker. The glove will improve grip as well as protect the left hand from wear and tear.

Another thing to consider is a golf pull cart. Don't think twice about pulling vs. carrying your golfer's clubs. In most cases junior golfers are required to walk the course during play. Some exceptions are local rules where the junior can ride in a cart between holes. You will have a lot to think about, especially at the beginning. Make it as easy as possible for you. A pull cart will also come in handy for the tournaments where you are not allowed to caddy. The cart allows your golfer to carry water, an umbrella for sun and rain protection, and a towel. Some courses have pull carts available; ask if you don't have one.

A tee is used to tee up the ball at the start of every hole. Tees are not allowed during play other than on the tee box. A good rule of thumb is to use a tee that allows the ball to tee up with half the ball above the club. Some tees are marked or shaped to help set a specific ball height. This is an individual preference and easy to try. A bit of nostalgia: in the old days, tees were made with little piles of dirt.

Another thing to have is a ball marker. The marker is used on the putting green. The green is the only place a player can always lift, clean, and replace their ball. Often, another player will request your player to mark their ball. Marking the ball is where you carefully place the marker directly behind the ball (the side opposite the hole), then carefully lift the ball. You should read more about ball marking in the USGA rules. There are nice markers available for sports teams and themes etc. all adding to the young golfer's excitement about the game. One essential tool is a marker pen for writing and/or drawing an identifying mark on the ball. This identification mark is important to help affirmatively identify a ball in play. Every player needs to mark their ball for this purpose.

A very useful, but optional piece of equipment is a distance device, or range finder, of some sort. There are generally three types: 1. an optical scope, 2. a laser scope, 3. a GPS mapping device. The optical scope has no electronics; it uses lenses like a telescope to measure distance. Usually you look through the view finder, and the height of the flag pin will indicate the distance to the hole. Flag pins are a standard height and the reticule in the view finder is calibrated so the height of the flag shows the distance. Laser range finders use laser technology to send a beam out to the pin then receive its reflection back to measure the distance. The third type, GPS or Global Positioning Satellite, is used to map the course and show you a picture of each hole and your location along with other features on the hole like hazards and trees. Be aware that devices that measure slope angle, or the elevation, of the hole, or wind, are not permitted for use in most tournaments.

Chapter Twelve – Daddy Caddy, and Mommy Caddy Too

Golf is different from the Osmosis Sports in another way. For most sports, the parents stay on the sidelines and there is a coach-to-child ratio of perhaps one or two to twenty. In golf, in most cases, there is a one-to-one coach-to-player ratio. As caddy for a young golfer, you are their coach. What a fantastic way to spend time with your child. Aside from perhaps target shooting, I can't think of another sport where you get to work as a team like this with your child. Most other times, unless you coach, you are a spectator. Caddying with my son on a beautiful golf course has given me some of my greatest memories.

However, do not underestimate the challenge of this role. Every dad and mom who has caddied for their child and reads this will be immediately nodding their heads … caddying for a child golfer can be a real challenge! If we all didn't invariably have to run to support other children's activities, or do our honey-do list, the nineteenth hole (the clubhouse bar) would be full of daddy caddies, and mommy caddies, after every tournament. The dads often joke that there should be a therapist standing by for us after every round. Please be sure though, caddying for your child can be one of the most fun and heart-warming things you can do, when you approach it the right way.

When you decide to caddy for your golfer, you make a commitment to act as their assistant, cheerleader, agent, parent, and finally coach. This commitment is not unlike coaching in any other sport. In fact, most coaches for young athletes understand this well, and you do too if you've volunteered to coach for children before. If you haven't, then it's important to understand that is your role as caddy. You are their coach during play.

Before I give you some nitty-gritty on being a child golfer's caddy, I want to share with you one thought. Perhaps the most important component to your role as caddy is by far the role of parent. Your oversight as a parent must guide the string of circumstances leading up to any shot, hole, and even tournament. Which events to play must be checked by the parent's view of priorities such as school work, family, or even faith commitments; many tournaments are on the weekend. How to handle your child's behavior after her bad shot is best governed ultimately as a parent. How to handle your child's reaction to another player's potential penalty or behavior is best governed ultimately as a parent. The values and lessons you want your child to learn will have plenty of "face time" during the course of becoming a golfer. Parent is job one.

Remember, we are talking about a four year old, or a seven year old, etc. At the end of the day they are children. Therefore, the potential for: crying, tantrums, cheering, trash talking, banging clubs, throwing balls, lack of focus, distractions, dissention, arguing, disappointment, and even disinterest, is real. There are many different types of children and you will see them all out there. Even some who seem to be the dream kids, the perfect young golfer, often have their challenges. There are many types of parents too, and you'll see them all on the course. The big challenge for some parents is to always remember to decide and act as a parent out there. Sometimes that's not what's best for the score. Golf offers a lot of opportunity to learn integrity for example. As a parent, teaching your child to focus on their own game and calling their own penalties may be a better lesson at this age than to allow them any focus on another player's penalty on a particular stroke. The tournaments you play will be a lot easier when you play with caddies who prioritize the parent component of their role as caddy. We were once paired with a 10-year old girl and her dad was caddying. My son and I watched her mark and lift her ball properly on the green. The ball was in a "brown" slightly rough patch on the green. However, when she replaced her ball, she placed it nearly 3 inches closer to the hole in front of the marker and out of the brown patch. This situation is one of the challenges the daddy caddy will face in your child golfer's tournaments. Should you say something in the nicest possible way, which technically is the "right golf" thing to do, or, just let it go, teaching your golfer to stay focused on their own play? Well my son said something. He is pretty sharp. Unfortunately, her daddy caddy decided to say, "She is fine, it's okay." Now, the young girl, my son, and I, all knew what she did. You may or may not "fault" the young girl. However, the lesson her dad taught her could haunt her for the rest of her golfing career. He taught her it's ok to break the rules if you can. I suggest he missed a great opportunity.

I am happy to tell you that I learned A LOT over time as a daddy caddy. I credit my growth and improvement as a caddy to my willingness to learn and be reflective, to keep focused on my role as a parent over that of assistant, cheerleader, agent, etc. I now always try to give priority to what the parent should do as that is what matters most, not the score on any given round for an eight year old. It was admittedly hard at times, but my growth also enabled noticeable improvement in my son's game. Now you and your golfer may have the perfect storm of traits needed to be just awesome on the course, and if that is so, congratulations and go on and skip ahead. My experience tells me otherwise though. The variety of children, parents, and ages, brings different challenges.

A four year old golfer is much different than a ten year old golfer. At the age of four or five years, after parent, the next important role is technical assistant. At this age most of the players seem to need more help with the basics like specific club selection, grip, and alignment. They are generally not able to relate a yardage to club selection. They will need your help. So, the caddy's function will be to hand the right club to the golfer, teach them the selection, and ensure a good setup, alignment, grip, and swing.

It's a tough race between assistant and cheerleader next. The reason I didn't put cheerleader in front of assistant is the significance of having fun. Despite our best intent, the fun can be directly proportional to the outcome of each shot. There is no denying it, the better the golfer is doing, the more fun everyone is having. That's where cheerleader comes in next. At this young age, it is especially important that your child golfer has fun. Even at the expense of outcome. They will not put emphasis on the outcome like the grown-ups do. That means that letting him chase the duck near the hazard for a minute, could be worth more than you think versus reeling her in to focus on the shot. Golf course = fun is a good thing.

At eight, nine, and ten, the players start to become more independent; some a lot more than others. They can, should, and will start to relate distance to their own club selection. So your help may shift to giving them the distance instead of giving them the club. In this age bracket, they will likely start to determine the distance themselves using the course markings or a range finder. Many will ask for confirmation of club selection and alignment. The more successful caddies start to back off as assistant at this stage and more on to coach and cheerleader.   One note, constructive criticism and observations of what caused an error are very often received as just criticism at this age and may need to be handled gingerly, depending on what type of personality your golfer has. Be careful, despite your best intentions, the independent ten year old will blame the caddy for bad alignment, or the wrong club, or get mad if you tell them where their setup went wrong. This type of reaction can affect the next few shots. I've seen and experienced this frequently. Letting it go and accepting "the blame" many times is the fastest way past the little golfer's temperament and putting the error behind both of you. The middle of a tournament is not the time to be teaching.

Recall that agent is mentioned as one of your roles as caddy. Junior sports are flush with stories of the over-the-top parent. We've all seen video of the dad running out from the sidelines and tackling a child in a recreational football game because he didn't like the way his son was hit. Those parents are quickly labeled and do not represent their athlete well. Golf has its share of these parents too. Honestly, I was looking down this road early in my caddying days, giving priority to each moment, each shot, what the other players were doing, the outcome. Fortunately I have a good friend, a very smart friend with lots of sports experience through college play. When I discussed this challenge with him he helped me adjust my priorities and I am grateful. Our experiences improved almost immediately.

Hopefully you are open to understanding your challenges when it comes to watching your child in competition. Things don't always go the way you'd like in sports, that's just part of the game. It's okay to be challenged like that and it's more common than you may want to believe. Different folks handle it differently. Most parents are better than others at not taking things too seriously. Keep your parent role as priority and push bad calls, bad shots, and any negative reaction way down in priority. Winning should not be a priority. Setting the best example of sportsmanship, respect for the game, respect for the officials, respect for the course, respect for the rules, and respect for the competitors, are all the best things you can teach your child golfer for the long haul. She'll likely grow up as a golfer with all the players at this age as the years roll on, and representing her this way now is perhaps the best thing you can do for her game.

Any good children's coach will tell you the best focus is on effort, not outcome. Unless you are just hell bent on having the next world number one, focus on effort, not outcome. In fact, I would argue that you have a better chance at world number one focusing on effort more so than outcome at this age. The good news is, your child golfer will likely not easily correlate any specific moment during the round, and what he does at that moment, to the outcome on the leader board at the end of a round. At this age they just don't have the cause and effect development to do that. In any given moment, compliment effort, reward improvement. For example, my son was challenged by doing his routine for every shot. He would seem to always rush right up and take a swing. So instead of setting a score goal, we set a number of times he did his routine goal, and reward. This allowed us to focus on his effort to do his routine. Of course the outcomes (scores) improved as his routine improved but our focus was on the effort.

Over time, the daddy caddies all develop their own little system for supporting their child golfer during tournaments. Think about your own system that works for you. I always enjoy prepping my son's bag the night before a tournament. I clean his clubs using an all-purpose cleaner, brush, and rag; I read somewhere that clean grooves are important. Make sure he has an ample supply of tees and balls. I would mark a few balls as well and have them ready. Double check the batteries in the range finder. Check the weather and prep the rain gear as needed. Make sure his ball marker was there; this always seemed to wander off on the hat it was last mounted to. Check the pull cart. Clean his shoes. Being prepared the night before allowed both of us to start the day easily and relaxed. We just simply needed to put the bag and cart in the car and go.

We sprung for an umbrella holder on our cart. Here in South Florida, this is a valuable accessory, not as much for rain as for sun shade. Sun screen is a must and bug repellant is often handy to have. Keep in mind that many clubs and tournaments have sun screen and bug repellent at the starter if you forget. Yes this is all your responsibility as daddy caddy too.

Upon arrival at the course we check in, apply sun screen, warm up on the range, warm up on the green, and head to the first tee ten to fifteen minutes prior to our tee time, as per the usual tournament director's request.

Chapter Thirteen – Nutrition, Rest, and Scheduling

After about fifty tournaments I realized I was meeting three different kids during a nine-hole round. My son was the player there the whole time, but he seemed to be a different child for the first four or five holes, another child for holes five through seven, and then another for the last two holes. The difference was more or less noticeable on any given day. His sensitivity and the potential for tension between us invariably spiked around hole five or six. This was a problem for both of us, and for mommy spectator too!

For the first few holes things would be pretty normal. We both would seem to be settling into and enjoying the round. The social aspect of interacting with the other players in his pairing was always exciting to him for the first few holes and that is what most influenced his behavior. You could say we were sort of on autopilot for those holes. Then almost like clockwork, around hole five or six, he would have an extra-negative reaction to a bad shot. Any comment or attempt to help from me was invariably met with anger as a criticism, no matter how hard I tried to present what I saw and thought nicely. Then as if by magic, he would settle down and really seem to be guided by the best of the early holes and the middle holes; having fun with focus and good effort, and all was forgotten and forgiven.

Other daddy caddies would reveal they had similar challenges throughout a round. After I became aware of this phenomenon, I observed others more closely and could in fact see very similar behavior. This was "more true" for some, and less for others, depending upon the child and parent. Even one of the most focused players on a tour revealed this behavior once when we were paired with him, and this is one focused little guy. We were not alone.

Chance would have it that right about this time, our coach and PGA Pro Rusty Baciagalupe recommended a book called <u>Eight Traits of Championship Golfers</u> by Dr. Debbie Graham and James Stadler. Well, I did some research and was able to find a phone number for Mr. Stadler and he so graciously called me back. When I told him about my observations, thinking I needed to get Dylan a sports psychologist, he immediately asked about nutrition and in particular the use of "sports drinks".

Like virtually all the other players, a sports drink was a staple in our cooler and starting on hole one, concerned about hydration, my son would start drinking it. I learned on that fateful call that the sugar content of sports drinks is much higher than I thought. My son was crashing from a sugar rush like clockwork right around hole six and rebounding at hole eight! We would pack Gatorade®, chocolate covered almonds, grapes, oranges, and fish crackers; way too simple-carbohydrate rich. We put a different nutrition plan in place and saw immediate results. I mean it was almost magic. He was one child again. His behavior was very flat throughout a round and we got along much better in the middle. Needless to say his score dropped as well and he rose on the leader board.

We switched to a sugar-free sports electrolyte powdered mix and water, minimal carbohydrates (maybe crackers or pretzels as he was not a big vegetable eater despite our best efforts), more protein from nuts and cheese, and kept the grapes and oranges. We always tried to keep protein in his breakfast as well to start off in balance. He would have only water for the first three holes. On hole four we would switch to the electrolyte mix of a pack in a bottle of water with half a pack of sugar free drink lemonade drink mix like Crystal Light®. For snacking, only nuts or cheese for the first half of the round and then grapes or oranges were ok to add for the second half. He liked the Gatorade®, or an Arnold Palmer, so those were only allowed at hole nine.

Another thing we always tried to do was have a good night's sleep and leave plenty of time in the morning for morning things to happen as needed. The sleep is very important. You are asking a seven year-old to stay focused for forty or so golf shots for more than two hours. That's not easy, and even harder if they are not well rested. Be sure to give them at least eight hours of sleep. We noticed a marked difference on the occasions where we did not honor this rule.

In the morning, it's important to leave time for a good unrushed breakfast and potty duty if needed as well. For example, say we had a tee time of 9:00 am an hour away. We would always plan to be at the course one hour prior to our tee time. So working backwards, we would plan to arrive at 8:00 am, which meant we would leave at 7:00 am and that meant we would get up at 5:30 to 6:00 am to leave a comfortable hour-plus for the morning stuff.

We don't know what our son's golfing future will hold, but we do know that the adjustments we learned and made will be good for him for a long time. We also know that our priority role as parent first has been well served.

Chapter Fourteen – Some Technical Observations and Suggestions

Let me begin here by repeating that I am not a PGA Professional, nor even a really good golfer for that matter. If I tracked it my handicap would be around twenty-five, though I hope to improve. What I am however is a student of golf and the golf swing. More specifically a student of helping my child become a better golfer and more helping our family truly enjoy the wonderful moments golf has given us. So, the observations and suggestion I make all come from that perspective; just a regular dad with a talented son who only wants the best for him. I will always maintain a deep respect and support for the value of a PGA Professional. I suggest you do the same and get one to help you however you can. While our time and budget allowed, our child golfer went to lessons with a PGA golf pro.

I feel compelled to offer what I observed about the technical parts of a golf swing and play as a daddy caddy. There is value there, and this is not a golf instruction book, it's a parent's guide to help their child golfer. I only hope to set the stage for you to help your child golfer knowing her as no one else can.

First I want say that at the early tournament ages of four to eight, straight beats distance every time. The players with the best scores at this age are the ones who hit the ball straight every time. The length of the nine-hole course may be only 1500 yards or so. With par fives only two-hundred yards long, there is always enough club for the next shot. Focus on improving the ball contact and accuracy of your child's shots at this age. Don't worry about distance. This means you can abbreviate their swing and teach them to swing easy and not think about "hitting" the ball, but just swing easy through the ball. Start to develop their tempo. He used to think *peanut* in his back swing and *butter* in his through swing.

I always told my son that his number one job out there is contact with the ball. Everything he does is to make good contact with the ball. That is his single most important swing thought. Good contact with the ball almost always means a better next lie to work with, kind of like billiards. There are four major parts to a golf swing: setup, back swing, through swing, and finish. Every section must support the number one goal of good contact, even the finish. Thinking about swinging to a good finish definitely affects the swing on the way there. The finish is very important.

The next thought was, "head down and look at the ball." Adults' instructors will have varying thoughts on this and it's up to you and your pro to ultimately decide, but for a young child simply telling him to keep his head down looking at the ball until it is gone seems to be something they can handle and along the right idea. For many pros, I noticed their head is down at the ball until their club is pointing at the flag, and then starts up. Another thought to consider is "keep your head quiet", in other words, your head should not move too much during the swing.

The next swing thought was, "trophy finish", as I mentioned earlier. A good balanced, stand up, forward finish is absolutely critical to a sound golf swing. I learned that staying behind the ball at address and during the swing is an important part of a fundamentally good golf swing. One observation is that a lot of children quickly develop what is called a reverse tilt. A reverse tilt is where their head actually bends towards the flag during the backswing. I think it comes from the natural tendency to try to hit the ball. The reverse tilt is a hard habit to break and causes a lot of shot inconsistency. Thinking about a good stand up and forward "trophy finish" makes it harder to have a reverse tilt in your back swing. I snuck in a slight shoulder tilt right and the famous Jack Nicklaus slight right chin turn when my son was seven to help this as well.

Later at seven, eight and older, distance becomes more important. By the time they are ten and eleven, distance is very important as they will start to see eighteen-hole rounds of more than 5000 yards. Some of the players who were on top in the early years start to creep down the leader board at this age due to distance. Some par fives reach over 400 yards and the smaller, though straight, players start to struggle versus the larger children who have found distance. Some ten year olds drive 250 yards and more! Of course a good foundation of accuracy remains critical to the game forever. Contact is job one.

Since distance becomes important, the independent, and proud, ten year olds will start to talk about "crushing it." This thinking is good, but introduced a challenge with keeping tempo in the swing. Most golfers will tell you consistency will suffer the minute you start thinking about killing the ball. A wide, smooth, fast through swing for the driver is the goal. Club head speed, more than power, generates distance. A swing thought I learned to keep his tempo is, "soft hands". I saw Tom Watson once show how to hold up a club with the head pointing at the sky and loosen your grip until the club just nearly slides down. He said, "This is all the grip you need." I taught my son this and we used the "soft hands" thought to remind him.

Soft hands is also a good thought for putting. A good smooth controlled stroke is important for good putting. A great drill I learned to keep my son from banging the ball when putting was to put a coin on top of his putter. Keeping the coin on the putter throughout the stroke teaches a nice controlled putter stroke. This drill also taught him that the back stroke is the same size as the through stroke and to putt further in most cases you simply increase the back stroke, not hit the ball harder. Another thought for putting is once you have the line, putt the ball for distance to finish close to the hole. No three putts. Trust the line, putt it close, and hold the finish. Finish the putter stroke with the putter pointing at their target and hold it for a three count minimum. Teach your golfer to believe in their finish and hold it. Bailing out early on any shot, including putts, will have inconsistent results.

At any age, the better golfers have a routine for every shot. The routine is important for your child golfer. Forcing a routine on my son didn't work nearly as well as when he finally designed his own routine. Once he designed his own, he owned it, it was his, and his game improved. The routine will likely be slightly different for putting than for the other clubs, so keep this in mind.

A word about sand bunkers. For every other iron shot, the goal is to hit the ball first and then the ground. This is not the case for green-side bunkers (though it is true for fairway bunkers in general). In the sand trap, teach your golfer to set up with the ball slightly forward of the center of an open stance, open the club face, and take a normal full swing back and through. However, she needs to swing down and through the sand about two inches behind the ball. Don't cheat the through swing, or the backswing, make them smooth and full to a balanced finish. Keep the club moving through to finish.

Getting down and through the sand is critical. In practice I would make a mark in the sand with the club two inches behind the ball and teach Dylan to focus on getting "the sand ball", not the real ball. I actually had to have him exaggeratedly hack at the sand in the bunker hard and repeatedly to get comfortable with hitting down and through the sand. Taking too much sand at this learning point is better than too little a she risks blading the ball thin. Another thought we used was a clock, making sure he swung from three o'clock, "get six o'clock", to nine o'clock. Get six means down, into, and through the sand.

Hitting the ball thin in a bunker is your worst enemy as the ball will fly across the green and invariably into the bunker on the other side. I can't tell you how many times I watched a child golfer, including my own, ping pong back and forth between bunkers. The goal is for the ball to fly up onto the green on a small pile of sand about the size of a donut. Work on the bunker; repetition breeds confidence.

For short chip shots, feel comes from practice. The biggest challenge I observed in the child golfer is a tendency to cheat the finish and sort of hack it, this will yield inconsistent results. This stroke is similar to putting in that the length of the back stroke determines the distance of the shot, not hitting with different strengths. Keep their weight forward (left for right handed players) and be sure to have a balanced forward finish. To drive the finish home, I used to make Dylan take a step or two toward the hole right after his finish. Making him think of finishing so he could immediately walk to the hole forced him to finish forward and balanced.

Just to recap, here is an easy list to refer to:

• Routine,
• Good contact is job one,
• Swing easy, "peanut butter"
• Head down and look at the ball,
• Slight right chin turn (left for lefties),
• Keep your head quiet,
• Soft hands, for all clubs, putter too,
• Trophy finish,
• In a bunker, hit the sand, "get six",
• Walk to the hole, after chipping.

As I mentioned, this is not intended to be an instruction book on golf. There are too many more qualified guys out there who write those books. Please take what I suggest here for what they are; from observations made while watching my son's golf game evolve during his young years. I am simply repeating what I have learned from the teaching pros. I have seen enough child golfers to know that what I am suggesting is not far off, but I suggest you get the help of a PGA pro to filter the above appropriately for your young athlete.

I do want to mention something I think added a lot of extra practice time on the green. Putting is critical to lower scores. If you haven't heard already, "drive for show, putt for dough;"

cliché but true. We used to play the good ole' basketball games of PIG and HORSE on the putting green. We still play them today. In case you don't know how to play PIG, let your golfer go first and pick a putt to attempt. If he makes the putt, the other player has to make the same putt, else earn the letter P. The first one to PIG loses. HORSE is the same, just spell horse instead of pig. Always keep fun in the picture. We also had chip and putt contests, closest to the pin contests, and in fact, he was beating me in nine holes by the time my son was nine.

Chapter Fifteen – What's Next?

When your child golfer reaches middle school age you'll start to think more about Junior Golf versus child golf. If your child golfer has taken a liking to competition, there are many great opportunities to do so. Many of the tours provide flights for older children up to age thirteen, fourteen, and some to eighteen. These tournaments are great fun to watch as the players at this age "get all serious" about their game. Many have sights on playing for high school teams, college, and even turning pro. You'll be amazed at how well these junior golfers play, and how far and straight they can drive!

Hopefully your middle school can support a golf team. The nice thing about school golf is that it brings a team component to the game. The team flavor is largely missing from golf, as it is mostly an individual sport. School teams add wonderful teamwork and social components to the game for your junior golfer. School golf is scored on team points so each player can contribute.

The PGA has initiated the PGA Junior League Golf program which is enjoying some success. Look for a PGA Professional near you and they will certainly be able to point you to a team. Many PGA chapters have junior tours as well. Look for the

AJGA® and other organizations like Hurricane Junior Golf Tour. These junior tours are feeder competitions for college golf. If you're interested in college golf, score starts to matter now.

Your now junior golfer will be very independent. Expect to retire the Daddy Caddy cap and bib and be relegated to spectator. This change was one of the most bitter-sweet revelations for us as child golfer parents. The transition happens as your "middle-schooler" is more independent anyway, but also many tours, and the schools don't allow caddies.

If you're reading this, you're likely not there yet so, enjoy the moment. Just be aware of your responsibility to one-day cut the cord. Actually, once you get passed the urge to coach, and get used to staying 30 yards away at all times, it's a new level of pleasure you will have watching your junior golfer compete. Some of the best pictures we have are of our golfer walking away down a beautiful fairway, chatting with his playing partners.

If competition is not in the cards for your junior golfer, there is every reason in the world to keep them playing this wonderful game. Play with them! There are few better memories you can build for you and your golfer than those on a golf course together. Staying in the game is a great gift for life, regardless of level of play.

Chapter Sixteen – Have Fun!

Some last minute pointers. Look for team match play tours now. Match play is a good way to add a bit of team work to golf. If you can't find a match play series nearby, try suggesting it to the local tournament director, they may like the idea. Be sure to check the PGA™ Junior League in your area too. Another possibility is group lessons or golf camp during holiday breaks from school and summer vacation. All of these are good ways to add more of a social component to golf that children always enjoy. Also keep in mind golf camps for the youngsters. During holidays and summer, many golf camps are available in different areas and they can be a great way to improve your child's game while they have fun.

Cherish the time you spend on the golf course with your child golfer, whether it is practice, fun play, or a tournament. You will realize great pleasure and memories from these moments. If you ever want to be really proud, once your child can play a round, take him out with "regular" people for a fun round. Most folks can't resist complementing the junior golfer who can play and watch her beam with pride when she realizes what she has. The accolades your young golfer will get while playing with mere mortals will be very encouraging. Keep in mind that very quickly they will be good little golfers. By ten, even younger, many of the players are nearly scratch golfers! It is really something to see.

Golf has become a significant part of my son's life and I believe plays a fantastic role in starting to shape who he is and will be. We have given him a gift. He has a great grasp of honesty and integrity, independence, friendship, effort and outcome, focus, resilience, and persistence. Golf brings a lot to the table for our son as we mix it in with school, family, faith, karate, music, other sports, and just being a kid.

If this book has done its job, you should now feel much more at ease about getting your child into this wonderful sport. Golf is the most widely played sport on the planet and teaches some great lessons. For most golfers, it's not about winning, but about constant improvement and best effort. Both of these are great lessons for every child to experience and learn. You will realize great pleasure watching or caddying time and again. You may even learn a lesson or two yourself. Watching your son offer his handshake after losing a play off, stick to it after a few bad holes, or even a fist pump after a birdie, will all be moments you won't forget. They are a gift for you. Have fun, it is a game!

Index

Notes